A STEP-BY-STEP

SIAMESE CATS

MARGE NAPLES

Photography: Apple Cross, Victor Baldwin, W. Crooke, Isabelle Francais, Lee Genet, Vickie Jackson, Dr. Robert C. Koestler, Larry Levy, The Photographers, Jeanne Singer, Sally Anne Thompson, Eloise I. Trosan. In addition, many of the informal photos that appear in this book were taken by Phil Morini, owner of Phil's Chez Chat. Humorous drawings by Andrew Prendimano.

Distributed in the UNITED STATES by T.F.H. Publications, Inc., One T.F.H. Plaza, Neptune City, NJ 07753; in CANADA to the Pet Trade by H & L Pet Supplies Inc., 27 Kingston Crescent, Kitchener, Ontario N2B 2T6; Rolf C. Hagen Ltd., 3225 Sartelon Street, Montreal 382 Quebec; in CANADA to the Book Trade by Macmillan of Canada (A Division of Canada Publishing Corporation), 164 Commander Boulevard, Agincourt, Ontario M1S 3C7; in ENGLAND by T.F.H. Publications Limited, Cliveden House/Priors Way/Bray, Maidenhead, Berkshire SL6 2HP, England; in AUSTRALIA AND THE SOUTH PACIFIC by T.F.H. (Australia) Pty. Ltd., Box 149, Brookvale 2100 N.S.W., Australia; in NEW ZEALAND by Ross Haines & Son, Ltd., 18 Monmouth Street, Grey Lynn, Auckland 2, New Zealand; in the PHILIPPINES by Bio-Research, 5 Lippay Street, San Lorenzo Village, Makati Rizal; in SOUTH AFRICA by Multipet Pty. Ltd., 30 Turners Avenue, Durban 4001. Published by T.F.H. Publications, Inc. Manufactured in the United States of America by T.F.H. Publications, Inc.

Contents

HISTORY AND STANDARD

HISTORY

It is fairly well established that the history of Siamese cats is vague at best. Records in Siam (now Thailand) are all but nonexistent. It is fairly well established that Siamese cats were originally owned only by the king and the royal family in Siam. Possibly the fable that they were sacred stems from the fact that they are born white—anything white was sacred in Siam.

One ancient book now on display in the Thai National Library in Bangkok is *Cat Book Poems* in which the "pale-coated" Siamese is described as having black feet, tail, and ears (a fairly accurate description of a Seal Point). Further, this cat is said to have red eyes. The blue eyes of the Siamese reflect a reddish glow—blood color—when the wide-open pupil is met with a flash bulb or a light in the dark. This book is believed to have been written between the years 1350 and 1750, and it is thought to possibly be the oldest book entirely about cats.

Several cats are believed to be native to Thailand, one of the most notable being the Si-Sawat, or Korat, seen in American shows today. This is a totally silver-blue cat with green eyes, and many believe our present-day Blue Point is descended from the Korat.

STANDARD

The following is excerpted from the Cat Fanciers' Association (CFA) Standard. Standards may vary from one cat association to another.

Siamese have a body of one color and "points" (tail, feet, ears, and face) of another. The color of the points distinguishes the varieties of the breed and gives them their names. Pictured is Grand Champion Terlin Starquest, a Seal Point, owned by Terry and Linda Little.

General: The Siamese cat is, in general, an elegant, svelte, dainty cat with long, tapering lines, giving an overall appearance of glowing, muscular vitality. The exotic contrast in the color between points and body adds to the striking appeal of this very loving animal.

Body: The body should be medium in size, and is a distinctive combination of fine bones and firm muscles. The body appears to be long. The shoulders and hips should continue the same sleek lines of the body. The hips should never be wider than the shoulders. Conversely, the shoulders should never be wider than the hips. This description is referred to as a "tubular" body. The abdomen must be tight.

Ears: The ears should be strikingly large, pointed at the top and wide at the base, and should continue the lines of the wedge-shaped head when viewed from the front.

Profile: The skull is to be flat. In profile, the appearance of a long, straight line is to be seen from the top of the head to the tip of the nose with no bulge over the eyes and no dip in the nose.

Eyes: The eyes should be almond-shaped, medium in size, neither protruding nor recessive. They are to be slanted toward the nose in harmony with the lines of the wedge and ears.

They must not be crossed. There is to be no less than the width of an eye between the eyes. A Siamese cat's eye color must always be a deep, vivid blue.

Chin: The chin and jaw should be medium in size. The tip of the chin lines up with the tip of the nose in the same vertical plane and is neither receding nor excessively massive.

Head: The head should be medium in size and in good proportion to the body. Viewed from the front, the head shape should be a long, tapering wedge. The wedge starts at the nose and flares out in straight lines to the tips of the ears, forming a triangle. There is no break at the whiskers. When the whiskers are smoothed back, the underlying bone structure is apparent. Allowance should be made for stud jowls in the male (stud) cat.

Coat: The coat should be short, fine textured and glossy, lying close to the body.

Paws: The paws should be dainty, small and oval, and should have five toes in front and four toes on the back feet.

Whether of show- or pet-quality, a Siamese retains the charm of its breed. This is a Lilac Point male.

Legs: The legs should be long and slim; hind legs should be higher than front legs. Legs must be in good proportion to the body.

Tail: The tail should be long, thin, and tapering to a fine point. It must not have a visible kink. This requirement is often referred to as a "whip" or "pencil" tail.

Body Color: The body color of a Siamese should be even with subtle shading. Allowance is to be made for darker color in older cats as Siamese generally darken with age. There must be definite contrast between body color and point color.

Point Color: The point color must be dense, clearly defined, and all of the same shade of color. The points are the mask, ears, legs, feet, and tail. The mask should cover the entire face, including the whisker pads, and should be connected to the ears by tracings. The mask should not extend over the top of the head. No ticking or white hairs should be in the points.

SIAMESE COLORS

Seal Points: The body should be even, pale fawn to cream, warm in tone, shading gradually into lighter color on stomach and chest. Points should be deep, seal brown. Nose leather and paw pads should be black.

Chocolate Points: The body should be ivory with no shading. The points should be milk-chocolate color, warm in tone. The nose leather and paw pads should be cinnamon pink.

Blue Points: The body should be bluish white, cold in tone, shading gradually to white on stomach and chest. The points should be deep blue. The nose leather and paw pads should be slate colored.

Lilac Points: The body should be glacial white with no shading. Points should be frosty gray with pinkish tone.

COLORPOINT SHORTHAIRS

Many people feel that Red Points, Lynx Points, and Tortie Points are Siamese. However, I feel they are actually hybrids, since Siamese were crossed with American Shorthairs to get the Red Point color and in the process, the other colors were developed. (This is not to say they are not beautiful cats.) Colorpoints have the same conformation as Siamese, differing

The color contrast of their coats and their litheness of form are but two of the appealing qualities of the Siamese breed.

only in color.

SIAMESE-RELATED BREEDS

Siamese cats have been used in developing many other breeds, namely, Balinese, Burmese, Himalayans, Havana Browns, Manxamese, Ocicats, Oriental Shorthairs, Si-Rex, Tonkinese, etc.

You really haven't lived until you've been owned by a Siamese. They are jealous, protective, sometimes independent. You have to be on your toes to figure out how their minds work. They are a never-ending source of humor and enjoyment.

PERSONALITY

You may wonder why there are far more Siamese owned today than any other breed of cat. The reasons are many. A Siamese cat has a marvelous personality. He is unbelievably intelligent, fastidious, demanding, thoroughly entertaining, interesting, loyal, understanding, gentle, compassionate, coy, capricious, amusing, sympathetic, and he has a vast capacity for love. Don't buy a Siamese unless you can give him a great deal of love, unless you have a keen sense of humor, unless you enjoy an active and mischievous cat.

A Siamese can rightfully be accused of posing; the expression on their face proclaims loudly, "Look at me, can't you see how beautiful I am? How can you possibly resist me?" They think up tricks to play on you. They bring you gifts, sit on your lap, and stare lovingly into your eyes, trying to communicate with you. When they are hungry they have been known to rummage through the trash (if they can get at it), find a carton that has contained their food or a paper plate they have eaten from, and bring it to you to show you what they want. A good description of the Siamese is that they are a cross between a monkey and a dog. They aren't, of course, but their actions do remind you of both. They are marvelous travelers, whether it be by air, sea, or land. They can be trained to walk on a leash

FACING PAGE:
A pair of Lilac Point Siamese, Luzerne's Lexington and Champion Luzerne's Peerless, pictured at nine months of age. Owner, Eloise I. Trosan.

and to use the toilet, which really is wonderful because one can then dispense with the litter box.

LIVING WITH A SIAMESE

Your cat will always be at the door to greet you upon your arrival home and will be ready to play or to talk over the happenings of the day. Yes, they do talk. After you have lived with one for awhile, you will understand what they are saying, and when you speak to the cat, he will answer you.

Siamese are very good as children's pets. The child must be taught to treat the cat with gentleness and kindness, of course. Siamese and dogs become great buddies if you take the time to get them acquainted.

TWO SIAMESE

It is true that two Siamese cats are more fun than one. I like to call them "community" cats. They love company: human, feline, or canine. They will entertain themselves, you, and your friends with their antics, and they will be company for each other when you have to be away. However, if you can only have one, by all means have the one. They are great creatures of habit and are very adaptable. If you must be away all day, they will curl up and sleep for hours, being ready to visit and play when you arrive home. They make very good apartment dwellers.

These Siamese kittens are grooming each other. Even as youngsters, Siamese are fastidious about cleanliness.

THERAPEUTIC BENEFITS

Much can be read about the therapeutic value of pets, for children, senior citizens, and everyone in between—they fill everyone's need to love and to be loved. They are aware of their owner's mood, be it anger, anxiety, happiness, depression, whatever. They are wonderful therapy for a sick child or a shut-in. They open up new social contacts for their owners, who

A charming pair of four-week-old kittens. Some people prefer to own a pair of Siamese so that the cats can be companions for each other.

love to compare the antics of their pets. They have uncomplicated loyalties. Pets can and do satisfy important psychological needs of people. Children learn responsibility for the care of their pets, and through this they also learn consideration for others. A pet can be a life-line to reality. A responsive pet never questions his owner. A Siamese cat can be all of these things in addition to furnishing entertainment, companionship, a sense of well-being, and an enhancement of his owner's sense of beauty and harmony.

13

SOME BELIEFS I WOULD LIKE TO EXPLODE!

"Siamese are Mean." Only someone who knows nothing about them could possibly say this. You will never believe their capacity for love until you own one. Unfortunately the sad exceptions that have given the whole breed a bad name are ones that have been mistreated and have defensively fought back. If a cat scratches, it is usually because he has been surprised and frightened or mistreated.

"Siamese are Sneaky." Actually, they tend to be bold rather than sneaky. You should hear a couple of them chasing each other down a hall or around a room, especially when everything is quiet. They sound like a couple of horses galloping through the house! They can, however, walk soundlessly when it suits their purpose. There is nothing sneaky about a Siamese!

WATCH CATS

When you know your cat, you will find him to be every bit as good as a watchdog, except, of course, much more quiet. If you are sitting quietly reading, and your cat suddenly comes to attention, listening intently, then goes over to a window, there is probably another cat or a dog outside; but of course, it could be a prowler, especially if the cat is softly growling. Siamese often wake their owners when a room is filling with smoke or gas. Recently, I read of a Siamese killing a rattlesnake that got into his home while his owners were away. And, upon occasion, I have noticed all my cats sitting still, staring expectantly at the door, and I have opened it to find that someone had, indeed, rung the bell—which was out of order!

SIAMESE ARE A CONSTANT SOURCE OF INTEREST

Definitely! They are exactly alike in many ways, yet each is a completely different individual. They all seem to prefer drinking water from a dish left in the sink or from a dripping faucet rather than from their own water dish on the floor. Particularly tasty to the Siamese is the water in a bowl of flowers, so much so that both water and flowers may be spilled!

Kittens and grown Siamese, when playing, will successfully surprise one another and when they do, both will jump straight up in the air! They will come down stiff-legged

Note the alert expression of this Siamese, Grand Champion Terlin Misty Star, a Blue Point. Owners, Terry and Linda Little.

Grand Champion Nor-Bob's Ann, a Chocolate Point female. Owners, Norma and Bob Salsman.

with all their hair standing on end. One will run away with the other in hot pursuit behind him. The first will suddenly flip over on his back and catch his pursuer off-guard, ending up in a very advantageous fighting position. Remember, however, they are only playing.

HOW TO FIND A KITTEN

Once you've made up your mind that a Siamese is *the* cat breed for you, there is still much to consider before you make your final selection. Do you want a household pet who will be a companion for you or are you interested in a show cat (and the world of cat competition)? Is pedigree important to you? The wise prospective cat owner addresses these questions before he makes his purchase.

SELECTION

I would like to suggest that you attend a cat show to see the different Siamese colors and decide which one you want. Talk to the breeders and let them help you decide whether you want a male or a female.

Naturally, most people think of their local pet shop as a source for purchasing a kitten; remember, however, that a pet shop cannot possibly stock a large selection of Siamese kittens at all times. If your pet shop does not carry the type of cat you desire, there are other places to look. One is a cattery whose business is breeding show-quality cats; such catteries may have kittens for sale.

You might ask a friend who has a Siamese where he obtained the cat. You can also consult the classified section of your telephone directory. (In my estimation, good quality kittens are seldom advertised in the classified section of a newspaper.)

Finally, another way to find the kitten (or cat) of your choice is to consult the various cat publications.

Some individuals sell kits at six to eight weeks of age. I feel that selling kittens this young is a very bad practice. Natu-

FACING PAGE:
This bright-eyed kitten is Miyo Mid-Nite Express of Saroko, a Seal Point male. Owner, Dr. Robert C. Koestler.

This Siamese, named Mandy, is purrfectly content in the arms of owner Terry Little.

rally, when a kitten goes to a strange environment, he may not want to eat for a day or so, and such a little one can be in serious trouble in that length of time. An ethical seller won't sell his kittens until they are three to four months old, by which time they have had their cat fever/rhinotracheitis/calici shots, and will be much better prepared to leave mother and adjust to a new home, new people, and different food.

WHAT TO LOOK FOR

A Siamese kitten should feel solid and heavy, yet should look lean and muscular. Never buy a kit with watery eyes or a runny nose. He may have only a temporary cold, but these symptoms may be danger signs. If you still want a specific kit which is displaying these symptoms, ask the seller to save it for you and to call you when the kit has fully recovered.

18

MALE OR FEMALE

If you are buying for a small child, or if you plan to raise kittens, then you will naturally be looking for a female. However, if you are looking for a pet and have no small children in your home, then a male would be your best choice. I have found males to be more intelligent, more loving, and more companionable than the females. However, they are more a pet for an adult.

Siamese are playful, inquisitive creatures who delight in exploring their environment.

INTRODUCING A KITTEN TO A NEW HOME

CARE

Usually upon its arrival at its new home, a kitten is subjected to fondling by each member of the family. Sometimes it is taken to a neighbor's house, where it receives more of the same treatment. The poor kitten is scared, confused, and quickly becomes tired. He finds himself in a strange place, all the humans around him are strange, and his mother, brothers, and sisters are nowhere to be found. He is offered food he never saw or smelled before, and he doesn't want it anyway. Don't be surprised if he jumps away, hisses, and runs off to the darkest corner he can find, refusing to come out.

When you are introducing a kitten to a new home, confine him to one room and make sure a litter pan and food and water are with him. Leave him alone until he becomes somewhat acquainted with his new surroundings. After a day or so, when he becomes accustomed to the new smells and noises around him, let one member of the family make friends with him, feed him, hold and pet him. After that, leave the door to his room open and allow him to venture out into the rest of the house, and to the people in it, whenever he is ready. He soon will be right at home. If the kitten refuses to eat or becomes listless, call the seller from whom you purchased him and ask what you may be doing wrong. He probably will be able to tell you, and the kitten will soon thrive.

If there is another pet in the house, let it and the new

FACING PAGE:
Your new Siamese can get along well with a dog,
especially if you supervise the first few meetings
between the two of them.

arrival get acquainted while you are with them. The other pet may claim squatter's rights and resent your bringing in what he feels is a replacement for him. However, after a few days of curiosity, their desire to play will assert itself and they will soon become fast friends. Don't be alarmed at a great deal of hissing and spitting. This is only natural, and usually is only bluff. An older cat will adopt a kitten and take care of it for you. And, as I said before, Siamese usually get along very well with dogs.

HAVE YOUR SIAMESE ALTERED

Whether you buy a male or female, have the cat altered. You will have a much better pet if it is altered, because then its mind is no longer on sex. The operation for a male is called "neutering," and it is minor surgery. The operation for a female is called "spaying" and it is actually major surgery. An unaltered male will "spray," to mark his territory, and to advertise to any female around that he is available. This spray has a very foul odor to it. The female Siamese in heat will scream for days until she is bred. She may also spray. She goes out of heat for a week or two, and is right back in again if not spayed. The male may even scream louder than the female. He will howl at every window and door in the house and will keep it up incessantly.

Believe me, if you want a good, companionable pet, have your cat altered. It is not true that a female should have a litter before being spayed. Cats do not need the experience of motherhood or fatherhood before being altered. A cat's sexual urge is instinctive, but it is stimulated by the sex hormones in the body. If this stimulus is removed before a sex-behavior pattern has been set by practice, there is no frustration built up. An altered cat does not automatically become fat and lazy. The only change is in the urge to mate, which is eliminated.

An unaltered male sires untold numbers of unwanted kittens if he is allowed to run loose. Quite possibly, these innocent little creatures will be drowned in a pond somewhere or left in the country to fend for themselves. They may even end up in some medical laboratory as experimental subjects. Personally, I don't want anything like that on my conscience.

A cat carrier and a mirror make great playthings for this lively trio of Siamese.

KEEP YOUR CAT INDOORS

If you really love your cat and want him to enjoy good health and a long life, plan to keep him indoors. If allowed to run loose, he could be lost, stolen, run over, poisoned, or mauled cruelly by another cat or dog. In areas where fleas thrive, your cat won't bring them into the house if he doesn't go out. Our Siamese are never allowed out, and they are all healthy and happy. We have one who is past eighteen years old.

POISONOUS PLANTS

Several house plants such as philodendron, rhododendron, African violets, mountain laurel, and dieffenbachia can prove poisonous to cats if parts of them are eaten. Some outdoor plants that are poisonous are oleander, amaryllis, narcissus, iris, English holly, English ivy, privet, castor bean, delphinium, sweet pea, hydrangea, impatiens, lobelia, poinsettia and

maidenhair tree. If you find your cat eating one of these things, try to take it out of his mouth. If he starts to act the least bit strangely, rush him to your veterinarian.

CHRISTMAS TREES

Cats love to pull the tinsel off Christmas trees and chew on it, and will invariably swallow some of it. This is very bad for them. Put unbreakable ornaments on the lower branches and the tinsel up high. Cats love the smell of a real tree and are very tempted to climb into it. The best practice is to keep the cat out of the room where the tree is unless you are with him. An even better idea is to buy a reusable artificial tree.

OTHER DANGERS IN YOUR HOME

Teach your kitten not to chew on electric cords. Cats especially love to do this when they are cutting their permanent teeth, at about four or five months of age. If live current is running through the cord, the danger is obvious. Cats also love to climb into a warm dryer with clean clothes in it. It is easy to close the door on the cat and start up the dryer again. Be careful not to let your cat out if you have just put insecticide spray on your lawn. This is poison, and your cat often will eat grass and ingest the poison, or he may lick it off his paws.

GROOMING

Brushing: Siamese don't need a lot of grooming. They do enjoy a daily brushing to get the loose hair out of their coats, and of course, they love the attention this gives them. Use a hard rubber brush, and be careful not to take out live hair.

Bathing: Siamese never really need a bath, but if you want to bathe your cat, get everything you will need together at the sink, including towels to dry him. A double sink is ideal. Run tepid water into both sides. Wash the cat on one side and lift him into the clean water on the other side to rinse him. Don't get soap in his eyes! I like to run the water into the sinks before I get the cat. Cats hate the sound of running water, and seem to spook when they hear it, or they realize what is about to happen and try their best to get away.

24

Be sure to get all the soap out of the fur. Put on a nice rinse if you wish. Place the cat in a big towel and rub him vigorously to get the water out of his coat. This can take two towels. Be sure to have a warm place to put the cat when the bath is finished. He will spend a good deal of time rewashing himself, but when it is all over, he will be proud and happy to be so nice and clean. Cats really love to be clean, as you already know. They do a remarkable job of keeping themselves clean.

Clip Claws: Clip the cat's claws about once a week. You can purchase a nail clipper especially made for cats at your pet store. Nip off just the tip end of the nail. Never, never get into the "quick" and draw blood.

Ears: Sometimes a cat's ears will need cleaning.

Your pet shop offers a wide variety of products that help make pet grooming a pleasant experience. Consult your pet shop dealer for help in selecting those grooming aids that will most benefit your cat.

Some cats exude a dark wax. Dip a Q-tip into a bit of oil and work it carefully into the many crevices of the ear. The cat won't be too happy about this treatment, but he will look better when you have finished.

Eyes: Quite often a cat will have a discharge that dries up at the base of his eyes. Take a soft tissue and gently wipe it away. This is usually not cause for concern, but if it becomes excessive, it should be brought to the attention of your veterinarian.

Teeth: Dry food given daily will help to keep the cat's teeth clean and free of tartar. I have read that wiping the cat's teeth daily with a Q-tip also helps to keep them clean. Some people tell me they use a child's toothbrush dipped in peroxide to clean their cat's teeth.

FLEAS

In frost-free and humid climates, fleas live all year long. Where it freezes, they are eliminated for the winter months. A cat should never be allowed to have fleas. Did you know that one flea can bite into the cat's bloodstream once every hour, twenty-four hours a day? Multiply that by a hundred or so fleas, and you can readily see how totally miserable the cat would be. If permitted to go uncontrolled, fleas can cause anemia in debilitated cats and young kittens. Fleas actually suck the cat's blood. They also transmit bacterial and viral diseases, as well as tapeworms and some protozoan infections. Fleas feed and breed on the cat. Their eggs fall off and develop into larvae and then pupae. Adult fleas live only ten days away from their host, but they can live from six months to three years on their host. Flea dirt is noticeable in the coat as small black specks. This is excrement from the flea, and is mostly made of up blood sucked from the cat, passed through the flea's digestive system, and finally eliminated as dried blood. A drop of water on these specks will "reconstitute" them and you will see the speck of dirt change rapidly into a small blob of blood. The flea eggs can be seen as small white dots among the black debris.

Fleas must be kept under control. A good thing to do is to put some flea powder on the cat in places where it is hard to lick off—remember, it is poison. Place it under the chin, be-

hind the ears, and on the shoulder blades. Sprinkle it liberally in the cat's bed. Sprinkle it around the house, in corners, under throw rugs, and so forth. Vacuum often, as you will be vacuuming up the fleas, flea dirt, eggs, and larvae.

The health of a kitten can be judged by its texture of coat, brightness of eyes, and general liveliness. These Seal Point kittens are owned by the author.

A variety of products specially formulated to help combat fleas and ticks is available at your pet shop.

EAR MITES

Ear mites complete their whole life cycle in the cat's ears. You can easily tell if a cat has ear mites. He will continually scratch at his ears and will have an obvious coating of debris inside the ear. These tiny mites are equipped with heavy arms with tentacles which burrow into the ear lining. If an ear mite infection is ignored, it will almost inevitably be followed by a bacterial infection of the ears, because bacteria find easy access to living tissue via the holes left by the mites. Such an infection can then spread deep into the ear and eventually penetrate the brain, causing convulsions and death. Ear mites are picked up by cats only from contact with already infected cats.

The best way to get rid of ear mites is to see your veterinarian, who will treat the ear and will probably send you home with some product to apply regularly to the ear until the infection is gone.

FEEDING

A kitten will need to eat three to four times a day. He is using a great deal of energy to grow and play. At seven to eight months of age, cut him down to a twice-daily feeding. If you are using 6½-ounce cans of prepared cat food, give an adult about a half a can at each feeding. It is also a good idea to give some dry food as a treat and to help keep the cat's teeth clean. Be careful when buying dry food. Look at the ash content and buy the one with the least amount of ash. Too much ash contributes to the onset of cystitis.

When a cat becomes a senior citizen—after about twelve years of age—he should be given several small meals a day. Cats should always have fresh, clean water to drink.

To keep the cat's appetite sharp, it is best not to leave food out between meals (even dry food) or to leave an unfinished meal in his dish. If your cat starts to put on excessive weight, protect his health by cutting back on the amount you feed. Avoid giving a cat between-meal snacks, as this can become a bad habit and can dull his appetite for his regular meals.

FOODS TO FEED

Commercial Cat Foods: This is a multimillion dollar industry. Cat foods are available in dry-packaged, semi-moist packaged, and canned forms, and they come in many different varieties and flavors. Cat nutrition pamphlets state that none of these foods are complete cat diets despite claims to the contrary, and they should not be fed exclusively.

Many cats become addicted to one particular commer-

FACING PAGE: Champion Nicholas Jay of Rocat, a Seal Point male, owned by Catherine Rowan.

cial cat food and refuse other foods. Such addictions eventually lead to serious medical problems. It is important for cat owners to stop their cat from falling into this nutritional trap by remembering the importance of variety in a cat's diet.

Again, the best advice that can be given is that one usually gets what one pays for. Cheap cat foods probably contain cheap, poor quality protein with a high ash and water content and a low caloric value. A cat fed such a food will be over-

If you have several Siamese, it's fine to feed them from one dish, but be sure to provide enough food. In general, Siamese are good eaters.

fed if he is to meet his calorie needs and at the same time will be undernourished.

Manufacturers who put fish in all varieties of cat food offered by them are suspect as to the quality of their product. The fish may be covering up an unpalatable, low grade, offensive base. In addition, the manufacturer is obviously capitalizing on the well-known tendency of cats to become addicted to fish.

The majority of cat food manufacturers, particularly the larger well-known companies, are constantly producing improved cat foods as they gain more knowledge of the cat's nutritional requirements from their own research testing facilities. Despite these advances, however, none of the commercial cat foods are complete diets, and until more knowledge is available to cat owners on nutrition, variety in the commercial cat foods

you feed your cat and in the total diet (to include organ meats and egg yolks) is recommended.

Meat: Although cats are carnivores (i.e., flesh-eating mammals), they cannot survive on meat-only diets. Cats fed only meat will be poorly nourished and, as meat is low in calcium and high in phosphorus, rickets and other skeletal disorders can result, especially in kittens.

Fish: Fish is an excellent food and most cats like it, but here again, it is not a complete diet. Care must be taken not to allow the cat to become addicted to fish or a specific fish-

A family of Siamese. Members of this breed enjoy warmth and comfort and oftentimes will single out a cozy spot for napping or relaxing.

Grand Champion Singa Concertina, a Seal Point female. Owner, Jeanne Singer.

flavored food. Fish should be cooked.

Vegetables: Vegetables are not necessary components in a cat's diet. They are not digested by the cat if they are raw, so if your cat likes a particular vegetable, limited *cooked* quantities of it can be fed.

Dog Foods: Cats' protein, vitamin, and fat requirements are higher than those of dogs, and for this reason, commercial dog foods are not adequate diets for cats on a long-term basis.

Baby Foods: Meat-type baby foods are nutritionally excellent for cats, but they are best reserved for use in old cats with poor digestion or sick cats that must be force-fed. They do tend to cause diarrhea in cats.

Bones: The chewing of bones helps to keep the cat's teeth clean and tartar-free, and they are a good source of calcium. If you give your cat bones, they should be good substantial bones. Small, sharp, pointed bones should be avoided. Chicken bones are soft and splinter easily. If they are swallowed, they could cause trouble in the digestive system.

Fats: Cats can tolerate large amounts of fat in their diet. Commercial cat foods are low in fats because they tend to turn the food rancid. A daily teaspoonful of cooking oil, bacon fat, or butter (unless your cat is overweight) helps to keep the cat's skin and fur in good condition.

The eyes of a Siamese are a vivid deep-blue in color. Pictured is Grand Champion Cannoncat's Abelard, a Seal Point male, owned by Virginia A. Cannon.

Liquids: As I said before, clean, fresh water should be available at all times. Cats eating canned foods do not need much extra liquid, but the dry and semi-moist foods increase the cat's liquid requirements.

Milk: Most cats do not drink milk, and it is not essential in their diet. Following weaning, some cats lack the en-

Petitfois The Incredible Hunk, a Blue Point male, pictured at three months of age. Owner, June Shatto.

zyme necessary to digest milk and will suffer from diarrhea if they drink it. Pregnant cats and kittens need milk or a calcium supplement. I suggest that they be given canned milk diluted with an equal amount of water.

VITAMIN SUPPLEMENTS

Although not essential if your cat receives a good, well-balanced diet, vitamins do help meet the cat's nutritional needs and help raise the cat's resistance to disease if his requirements are not otherwise being met. Pregnant and older cats particularly benefit from supplements. I have always felt that Siamese particularly need additional vitamin C.

HARMFUL FEEDING PRACTICES

Liver: Feeding an exclusive diet of liver, or even excessive amounts, will cause lameness and crippling due to the effects of excess vitamin A on bone structure.

Canned and Raw Fish: Feeding an exclusive diet or excessive amounts of fish, especially tuna, will cause steatitis. The fish used is usually the fat part of the tuna. Feeding excessive cod liver oil which has gone rancid will also cause steatitis. Feeding excessive amounts of raw fish can cause a deficiency of thiamine (vitamin B_1). The enzyme in fish that destroys thiamine is destroyed by cooking.

Egg Whites: Feeding excessive amounts of raw egg whites will destroy the essential B-complex vitamin biotin and will cause skin problems. Cooked egg whites are all right, but it is best to feed raw yolks only.

PROPER FEEDING

The proper feeding of your cat requires only a commonsense application of the above suggestions and a weekly expenditure within the reach of even the most modest budget. It is not advisable to make sudden changes in diet, as digestive problems may result. Gradually introduce a new food. If you are feeding your cat differently from these recommendations and the cat is healthy, do not worry because you are obviously meeting his nutritional needs.

These Siamese youngsters are oblivious to their mother's scrupulous efforts to groom them!

USE OF SCRATCHING POSTS

TRAINING

Cats do require some object upon which to condition their claws and to stretch their muscles at the same time. They will usually find a place to scratch immediately upon waking, so I would suggest that their scratching post be placed near where they sleep. Scratching posts are available in pet stores in great variety. There is usually a good display of them at cat shows. Buy a good, substantial pole to start with. A kitten won't need one that large, but he will soon grow up, and will utilize it from day one. Be sure the pole has a good heavy base so it won't tip over with the cat on it. The choices are many. Some are simple, and some are very elaborate. The poles can be easily re-covered with leftover pieces of carpet when they become too worn and ragged. I have found that the ones covered with indoor-outdoor carpet are totally ignored by the cats, as they need something they can get their claws into and this carpet is too closely woven. By all means, get something for your cat to scratch on. Otherwise he will use your furniture and you will be very unhappy with him.

TEACH TO RETRIEVE

Siamese love to chase balls. Crumple up a piece of paper and throw it for him. He will love to chase it. When he plays with it instead of bringing it back for you to throw again, go get the ball and throw it again. Keep doing this, constantly repeating "bring it," and within a half-hour or so, he will get the idea. After that he will wear you out trying to get you to throw the ball for him. A word of caution: don't roll up foil. After a

FACING PAGE:
Something—or someone—has captured the curiosity
of this kitten! Owner, Dr. Robert C. Koestler.

while, little pieces flake off, and it is very bad for digestion if the cat eats them.

TOYS

Many toys are available at pet stores. Ping-pong balls are ideal. They are light to bat about, and cats really do enjoy them. Cats also love little things made from pipe cleaners and, of course, catnip toys. Cats love to play in paper sacks. Try making a "castle" for them out of a good-sized cardboard box. Cut doors and windows in it and place it upside-down on the floor. This will entertain cats of all ages for hours.

TRAINING TO USE THE LITTER BOX

No training is necessary for this. The kit's mother has already trained him to use it. Just be sure that the kitten knows where it is. It is wise to keep it in the same place at all times. If the need is urgent, the kit may not have time to look for it if you have moved it.

There are several kinds of litter available at the pet store. Perhaps you should inquire from the seller as to which brand the kitten is familiar with. It would be best to start with that. Some people use newspapers in the litter pans. If a kitten

A Blue Point queen pictured a few days before delivering her litter.

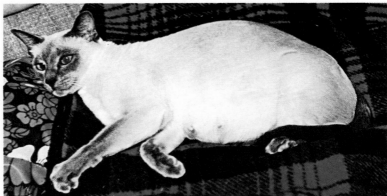

A pair of Blue Point Siamese kittens.

was used to that, he wouldn't know what litter was. The drawbacks to using paper are the odor and the possibility of the cat using any paper he might see lying on the floor. Some people use cedar shavings. These track all over the house. By far the best product for the litter box is commercial, deodorized, absorbent litter. Try to buy brands that are the least dusty. This litter is a bit expensive, but with only one cat using it, it can be stretched to last up to as long as a week. Lift out the solid material with a tool for that purpose, available at pet stores, and stir the remaining litter so it will dry. Siamese are very fastidious. They won't use a dirty litter box.

TRAINING TO USE THE TOILET

Training a Siamese to use the toilet is entirely possible

39

and is most convenient when accomplished, as it eliminates the necessity for a litter box. Some cats pick this up without any training. If you have one cat that uses this facility, any others you acquire will soon follow suit. One thing you must know before starting on this project is that the cat uses his tail to balance himself. Therefore, the cat must be sufficiently grown so that with his feet on a rim, his tail will reach across the opening. If you put the cat's litter box alongside the toilet, the cat may make the transition on his own simply by observing. Pet shops carry a variety of devices for toilet training your cat. What I did was make a little stool with a round hole in it that fit inside their litter boxes. The cats liked using this stool because they didn't get their feet dirty, and the transition to the toilet seat itself was very easy.

CARRIERS

I cannot stress strongly enough the importance of buying a carrier for your cat. There will be many occasions when you will need it. Pet stores have many varieties. Buy a good strong one that has plenty of ventilation. Those that stack are very handy. Always take your cat to the veterinarian in a carrier. We used to live next to our veterinarian, and it is very sad to realize how many cats panic in their owners' arms and get away and are never seen again. Another time a carrier is a necessity is when you are going to have your cat bred. She must be taken in a carrier to the cattery where the male lives, as she will probably become very upset when she sees all the strange cats and becomes aware of the strange smells. Don't buy a carrier just the size of your kitten. He will soon grow up and you will then need another carrier. Why not buy a big enough one in the first place?

VACATIONING WITH YOUR CAT

You will become so attached to your Siamese that you will want to take him on vacation with you, especially in the car. Siamese are great travelers! You may be surprised to notice how many people travel with their cats. On a long trip we take a small suitcase packed with just the cat's things. This contains quite a few cans of food, a water dish, paper plates for food, a

can opener, a spoon, a rubber brush, a flea comb, a harness and leash, a sweater, litter, disposable litter boxes, and a few clean towels for the bottom of his carrier. We always take a carrier along. There are times that you feel the cat is safest when confined to his carrier (for instance, when loading or unloading the car). It goes without saying that we only stay at motels or hotels where the cat is welcome. In addition, before letting the cat out in the room, we inspect it thoroughly to see if there are any hidden holes in the walls where the cat could squeeze through.

The term *svelte* is often used to describe the body type of a Siamese. Pictured is Grand Champion Chez-Chat's Wizard, a Blue Point male owned by Phil Morini.

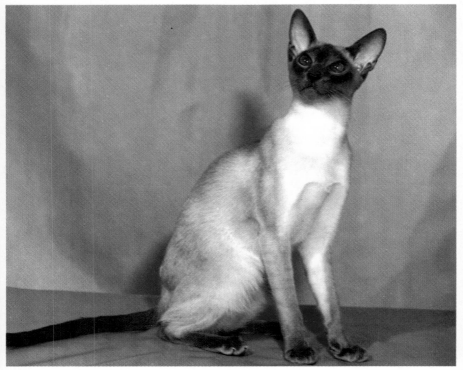

HEALTH

The best way to find a good veterinarian is to ask your cat-owning friends whom they use. You can always call your local Veterinary Medical Association—they won't recommend a veterinarian who has had valid complaints lodged against him. Ask the seller from whom you purchased your kitten what veterinarian he uses. There are good veterinarians and bad, sorry to say. Your veterinarian should be happy to explain things clearly and in non- technical language to your satisfaction. Other workers in the office should be courteous and confident in their handling of both clients and patients. Everything should be scrupulously clean. The veterinarian should be happy to discuss charges with you and should not hesitate to give you an estimate of whatever needs to be done. One sly little question you could ask is how many cats the veterinarian personally has. Sometimes a veterinarian will prefer dogs to cats. Don't hesitate to change veterinarians if you are unhappy with one.

IS YOUR CAT SICK?

This chapter is by no means meant to scare you. However, for the new owner, a little knowledge may mean the difference between life and death for his cat. It is natural for a cat to be in good health at all times. Many go through their entire life never having to see a veterinarian except for basic vaccinations (in case they weren't given before you purchased the cat).

Lack of appetite is a sign that your cat is a bit under the weather. Another sign is loose bowels. If he has what looks like a film over the corners of his eyes (this film is called a "third

FACING PAGE: The coat of a Siamese cat should
be fine-textured and glossy, lying close to the
body.

eyelid" or "haw"), and if it remains apparent, something is wrong. If the cat's coat becomes "tacky" or clumped together, and stands away from the body, this is a signal that all is not well. If he does not respond quickly to the suggested remedies for minor ailments, consult your veterinarian immediately. In good faith and ignorance, you can do great harm by treating the cat yourself, as many illnesses are closely related and have similar symptoms. Your best insurance for your pet is to promptly avail yourself of your veterinarian's experience and skill if anything seems abnormal.

HOW TO GIVE A PILL OR CAPSULE

Your veterinarian will often send medication home with you and instruct you on how to give it. The important thing is to be consistent about giving it for the prescribed time. In case of a pill, if you are right-handed, hold the cat's head in your left hand, open his mouth with the index finger of your right hand, and hold it open with the thumb and longest finger of the left hand. You will note a little groove formed at the base of the tongue. Drop the pill or capsule into the groove and give it a push into the throat with the index finger of your right hand. Transfer your left hand to the nape of the cat's neck and pull his head back while supporting his back and his hind legs with your right hand until he is upside-down. If all this is done quickly, he will be so surprised he will swallow the pill before he knows what has happened. You may find this procedure easier if you are seated and holding the cat in your lap. If he succeeds in spitting the pill out, hold him and pet him awhile. Then try again. In the case of capsules, it is helpful to coat the capsule with a bit of butter just before giving it. This will serve as a lubricant and the capsule will go down more easily. If you find this entirely too difficult, try crushing the pill in the cat's plate and mixing it with his food.

HOW TO GIVE LIQUID MEDICATION

Most bottles containing liquid medicine have a plastic dropper as part of the cap. These droppers can be boiled and kept in a clean place for future use.

To give the liquid medication, fill the dropper with the

Even though they might be fun to play with, many household plants are poisonous and therefore should be off-limits to your cat.

desired amount of medicine. Grasp the cat's head with the left hand in the same manner you would for giving a pill, and hold the mouth open a little way. With the right hand, insert the dropper at the side of the mouth and let the medicine flow slowly out of the dropper onto the cat's tongue. He has no choice other than to swallow the medicine. If the cat finds the medicine distasteful, he will allow as much of it as possible to drip out of the corner of his mouth. Have a tissue handy and wipe the mouth until it is clean while still holding the cat's head. Otherwise, he will shake his head and the medicine will fly in all directions.

With proper diet, regular veterinary checkups, and tender loving care, your Siamese kitten can grow up to be a healthy, happy cat.

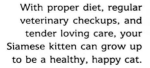

HOW TO TAKE A CAT'S TEMPERATURE

If you are going to take your cat to the veterinarian, it is helpful to take his temperature before you go, for often it will shoot up when he finds himself in the veterinarian's office. You should have a rectal thermometer at home for this purpose. Lubricate it with some petroleum jelly. Grasp the cat's tail at the base with your left hand while holding him against your side with your arm, and gently insert the thermometer in the rectum to a distance of approximately two inches. Leave the thermometer inserted for a full timed minute, all the while holding the cat to keep him quiet. When you remove the thermometer, read it before cleaning it. A cat's normal temperature is 101.5 degrees. Clean the thermometer with a piece of cotton moistened with alcohol, shake it down, and put it away. If a cat's temperature remains below or above normal for more than a day, something is wrong.

If you don't have a thermometer, and your cat's body

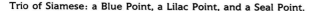

Trio of Siamese: a Blue Point, a Lilac Point, and a Seal Point.

In some cat organizations, cats with points other than seal, chocolate, blue, or lilac are called Colorpoint Shorthairs.

feels warmer than usual, and his paw and nose leather and his ears are very warm to your touch, he no doubt has a high temperature. He will also be listless and quiet. If a cat has a temperature, his body is fighting an infection. Conversely, if your cat feels cold to your touch, lose no time in getting him to your veterinarian.

47

In its first few months of life, a kitten will spend a good deal of time seeking out the warmth and security of its mother.

POISONOUS CHEMICALS

Many chemicals are poisonous to cats. Particularly dangerous are DDT, Chlordane, and Lindane in any form, such as insecticide powder or spray. Many coal-tar derivatives, such as those containing carbolic acid or phenol compounds, are equally dangerous. Lead, such as that found in paint, can poison your cat. Arsenic, usually found in weed killer or snail bait, can kill a cat. Read the label carefully to determine the contents of any product that your cat can possibly contact. Be especially careful of lawn sprays if your cat is allowed outside. Be very careful not to spray fly or odor-killing products where kittens can inhale the fumes. Kittens are very susceptible, and this could cause them serious harm if it doesn't kill them.

If you suspect poisoning, proper emergency treatment is to induce vomiting with repeated doses of one tablespoonful of a mixture of equal parts of three percent hydrogen peroxide and water until vomiting occurs. Try to identify the poison, and if possible, take the label with you to the veterinarian without delay. The label will indicate the antidote and save valuable time in administering treatment.

RINGWORM

Ringworm is a fungus, not a worm! It is the only common skin disease that can be transmitted from humans to cats and vice versa. This is no longer a serious problem if you get prompt diagnosis, obtain proper medication, and faithfully administer it. If your cat gets ringworm, you should diligently vacuum your rugs and scrub your linoleum floors after isolating the cat. The spores that spread the ringworm are carried in the fallen hair shaft.

If you keep your pet indoors, chances are few that it will contract diseases contagious to cats.

ECZEMA

Some cats are allergic to certain foods and their skin erupts into rashes and sores. Vitamin excesses or deficiencies can also result in skin conditions. Flea bites are a common cause of skin trouble. Certain flea sprays or powders may cause irritation. If the skin reaction is severe, an anti-allergy shot can be given to relieve the symptoms. Baths with a medicated shampoo will often soothe and help clear up skin inflammation.

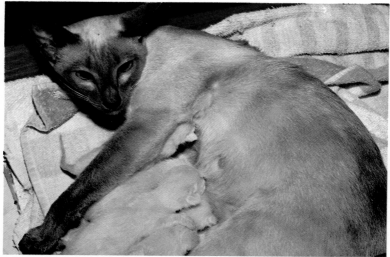

A mother cat's milk provides all the nourishment her kittens need in their early weeks of life.

BITES

A deep bite wound will seal over quickly on top. Outwardly the skin may show no break, but infection may be building up in the wound and throughout the cat's system. Treatment consists of lancing and injections of antibiotic. After that, remove the scab and clean the wound daily, as it must be kept open to heal from the inside out. Bites from insects can produce a severe reaction in some cases. Mysterious swellings may be due to insect-bite reaction and usually subside in a day or so. They may, however, require an allergy treatment.

A mother cat with a recalcitrant youngster in tow—a method of discipline that hardly ever fails to achieve the desired results!

TEETH—GINGIVITIS

A cat with a sore mouth will not want to chew or eat. This redness and soreness of the gums is called gingivitis. Teeth should be checked for tartar accumulations. When tartar is present, the teeth should be scaled to prevent irritation of the gums and infection. Infected teeth should be removed. Infection from abscessed teeth or roots can spread throughout the cat's entire system. After your veterinarian cleans your cat's teeth, keep them clean by brushing once a day with a small child's toothbrush, or swab the gums daily with a Q-tip lightly saturated in a three percent solution of hydrogen peroxide. If the gums remain sore and red, rub oil from a Vitamin E capsule on them once a day.

51

CYSTITIS

Cystitis is a blockage of the urinary passage and, if neglected, can cause uremic poisoning and a swift death. It is caused by a mucous plug forming in the urethra due to the irritation of a bladder infection. If you find your cat straining in his pan frequently, eliminating only a small amount of urine painfully, take him to your veterinarian immediately. Don't mistake this "straining" as constipation. Another cause of this condition is the urine being too alkaline. You can give your cat a little vinegar in his water, or some tomato juice in his food once or twice a week, to help keep his urine as acidic as it should be.

FELINE DISTEMPER (CAT FEVER)

This is a specific disease of cats which has no connection with dog distemper. It is a term used to describe any inflammation of the cat's intestinal tract. Kittens should be vaccinated against this deadly disease at an early age—preferably before they are sold. Onset of the disease is characterized by weakness, vomiting of a yellowish fluid, diarrhea, fever, and hanging of the head over the water dish. If an unvaccinated cat shows these symptoms, rush him to the veterinarian. The onset of death is often so swift that this condition is often mistaken for poisoning.

OTHER RESPIRATORY INFECTIONS

The symptoms of these diseases resemble those of a human's severe cold. The cat's eyes will water, his nose will run, his throat is sore, he coughs and sneezes and seems to be sore all over. He is feverish, listless and will not eat. He can have loose bowels. Several of these viruses have been isolated, and the rhinotracheitis/calici vaccines included in the triple shot kittens should be given do a great deal to control these viruses. If your cat has not had his cat fever/rhinotracheitis/calici shot, by all means have him get it at once. Boosters every year or two are beneficial in keeping his immunity in full force.

FELINE LEUKEMIA

Your cat should be tested for feline leukemia. If he tests positive, he should be isolated from other cats. If he is the

only animal you have, keep him indoors so he won't spread the virus to other cats. Some cats live out their lives with this virus while others die a few months after contracting it. There is now a vaccine on the market to protect your cat from getting this virus. You can check with your veterinarian regarding the advisability of having your cat vaccinated for this virus.

AIDS IN CATS

This is a very new feline virus that has recently been isolated in one colony of research cats. It is a very different virus from the human kind and is definitely not contagious to people. It is not yet known how this virus is transmitted. Much research needs to be done on it.

HAIRBALLS

Siamese seldom have this problem. If you suspect it, however, give him a little liver-flavored petroleum jelly (available under various brand names). Wipe some on your fingertip and apply it to the roof of the cat's mouth. He will have to eat it to get it off.

An expectant Lilac Point female.

BREEDING

Breeding is a very specialized field. Before you decide to breed your female cat (called a "queen"), you should consider what will be involved in time, effort, and adequate facilities both for the care and sale of the kittens. Please don't give the kittens away! If someone pays for a kitten, they will take far better care of it. If you decide to breed, keep in close contact with an experienced breeder who will be happy to guide you and help you find the right male for your queen.

WHEN TO BREED

Your queen will go into season or "heat" when she is anywhere from four months old to fourteen months old. There will be no doubt in your mind as to when she is in heat. She will "call" so loudly you will think she is screaming. She will roll on the floor. She will crouch and "pad" with her hind feet. She will lay her tail over to one side while padding. She will be extremely loving. If you pick her up she will stiffen in your arms.

It is not a good idea to breed a female before she is a year old, nor is it advisable to breed her in her first season; this is often a sort of half-season. Each queen will have her own cycle. Some females come into heat every few weeks, some every few months, and some seem to never go out until they are bred. You can easily see why, if you prefer to have her only as a pet, she is far better off if she is altered.

VISITING THE STUD CAT

It is customary for the queen to be taken to the stud. Decide which stud you are going to use before the cat is ready

FACING PAGE:
Double Champion Kim-Kee's Loki of T'lu, a Lilac Point. Owner, Janet R. Beardsley.

to be bred. Make arrangements with the breeder who owns the male. Agree upon the fee and upon whether or not you can have a second breeding, if the first one doesn't take, without paying another fee.

Take your girl to the male in a carrier. She may come out of season when she smells all the new odors and sees all the strange cats in a cattery. Leave her in the care of the breeder, and after a few days, she will be back in season and will accept the male. The breeder will call you and let you know when to pick her up.

WHEN TO EXPECT THE KITTENS

The breeder will tell you the first day your cat was bred. The usual time for the kits to arrive is 65 days after that. It is all right if they arrive a few days before or after that. Do not let your cat outside until you are sure she is out of heat. It is possible for her to be bred by a stray tom and for her to have kittens by two males. I have found that about half the time, a young queen doesn't "take" the first time bred. In this case, she would have to be taken back to the stud when she comes back into heat. At about three to four weeks, her nipples will start to increase in color and size. Then you will know she is pregnant. She will not require more food than normal, however. You don't want to feed her everything in sight, or the kittens may get too big. The kittens will be pure white at birth. They don't start to get color in their points until about two weeks of age. However, their eyes will open at approximately five days of age.

YOUR CAT WILL WANT YOU WITH HER

When the time gets close for the queen to deliver, she will dig in boxes, corners, and various secret places looking for a nest. Of course, you will have fixed her a box for that purpose, and you will have to insist that she use it. She will want you with her when she delivers. If you feel she is in trouble, don't hesitate to contact your veterinarian or the breeder.

RAISING THE KITTENS

The mother cat will take full care of the kits until they

These three-week-old kittens are eager to explore the world outside their nesting basket.

are approximately four weeks of age. All you have to do is feed her as much as she wants to eat and keep her nest very clean. When the kits are about three weeks of age, they will totter out of the box, explore, and attempt to play. They are darling, and you will thoroughly enjoy watching them. Soon they will try to eat their mother's food. This is fine. Sometimes breeders start them on a special diet of pablum and canned milk, but they will soon prefer the more tasty food their mother gets.

WHEN TO SELL THE KITTENS

You may decide to keep one or two of the kits, but the usual litter is four kittens (and can go as high as ten), so you won't want to keep all of them. The kits should have their cat fever/rhinotracheitis/calici shots before they are to leave. Many buyers like to have them tested for feline leukemia as well.

REGISTERING THE LITTER

Many people will be interested in having papers on their kitten. The owner of the stud cat should have given you his pedigree if you had it included in the price of the breeding. You should also have received a litter registration form signed by the owner of the stud. You will fill out the queen's part of the form, how many kittens there are in the litter, and what sex they are, and send it in to the registering body of your choice with the required fee. The name, address, and fee will be on the form. You will receive a "blue slip" for each kitten in the litter. Give one to your buyer, and he can send it in with his choice of name for the kitten and payment of the required fee for registering the kitten.

CATS MUST BE REGISTERED

The very first requirement is that your cat be registered to be shown. If the breeder gave you a "blue slip" when you bought the cat, you must have sent it in with your choice of a name for the cat. The breeder's cattery name precedes any other name. As an example, our cattery name is DiNapoli.

SHOWING

Let's say you want to name your cat Precious. The name would be DiNapoli's Precious. There can only be a total of 27 letters and spaces in a registered name. If you own a cattery, your cattery name would go on after Precious. For example, DiNapoli's Precious of Lowlands.

ENTERING THE SHOW

The first thing you must do is obtain an entry blank. Again, the breeder or a friend can help you do this. Fill it out and send it in to the entry clerk along with the entry fee. A confirmation will be sent to you acknowledging your entry. When the day of the show arrives, take your cat in his carrier and check in with the entry clerk, who will give you an entry number and assign you to a cage. You will furnish this cage with a floor mat and draperies best suited to showing your cat off to his advantage. He will be listed in the official catalog and will be judged by number only. When your number is called, take the cat to the judging ring and place him in a cage corresponding to his number.

SHOWING

Each show consists of four, six, or eight rings. Each

FACING PAGE: CFA All-breed Judge Donna Davis checking a Siamese cat's chin and jaw.

judge conducts a complete show independently of any other judge. There may only be All Breed Judges, which means the judge will judge every cat in the show; or there may be Specialty rings, which means the judge will judge your cat only against all the shorthaired cats. Most likely there will be a combination of both. If this is your cat's first show, he will be entered in the "Open" class. This class is for any cat that has not qualified for the Championship class. If your cat wins in his class, he will be awarded a red, white, and blue "winners" ribbon. This carries the championship points; the amount of ribbons needed for championship depends on what association is sponsoring the show. In the Cat Fanciers Association, he must win six of these ribbons to claim his championship. All of this gets very intricate, and you will not learn simply by reading or

Siamese relaxing in their show cage. The attached drape affords them privacy amidst the activities of a cat show.

While their owner is probably brimming with the excitement that a cat show creates, these Siamese seem unfazed by the whole affair!

even by attending one show—it will take several. After a cat is a champion, he earns "Grand" points. He must defeat a certain number of champions to qualify for Grand Championship. Each judge ends up choosing a Best Cat in Show. You will be very elated the first time you win this coveted award. People often have a Grand Party to celebrate when their cat has achieved this title. They serve an elaborately decorated sheet cake and champagne.

SHOW ETIQUETTE

A primary rule of show etiquette is never feed anyone else's cat without the owner's permission. A Siamese is never fed before he is judged for fear he may appear to have a pouch. It is a show rule to have your cat's claws clipped before the

Grand Champion Sin-Chiang Brandie of De Vegas, a Seal Point female, owned by Dan and Hanne Gauger.

show, and if this is not done, your cat will be penalized. Never take a cat to a show if he is coming down with anything. If you have small children, try to make arrangements for them to be cared for the day of the show. Small children running through the show hall are very distracting to the cats, the judges, and other exhibitors. Besides, the children get very bored and tired as the long hours drag on.

If you have won rosettes at previous shows, they must only be displayed inside your cage. Only rosettes won at the current show can be displayed on the outside of the cage.

AGE TO SHOW

No kitten is allowed in the show hall under the age of four months. Kittens are shown from four months to eight months of age. At the age of eight months they are considered adults.

The following books by T.F.H. publications are available at pet shops everywhere.

CAT CARE by Dagmar Thies (KW-064)
Presents sensible, easy-to follow recommendations about selecting and caring for cats. Illustrated with full-color photos. Hard cover, 5½ x 8″, 96 pp.

SUGGESTED READING

KITTENS by Kay Ragland (KW-019)
For kitten and cat lovers. Presents practical information about the care of kittens. Completely illustrated with full-color photos and drawings. Hard cover, 5½ x 8″, 96 pp.

ENCYCLOPEDIA OF AMERICAN CAT BREEDS by Meredith Wilson (H-997)
An authoritative, up-to-date book that covers completely the American and Canadian breeds. A highly colorful book that is a must for cat lovers and breeders. Illustrated with full-color photos. Hard cover, 5½ x 8″, 352 pp.

SIAMESE CATS by Ron Reagan (KW-062)
For cat lovers of all types, this book has its greatest degree of appeal to owners or potential owners of Siamese cats. Completely illustrated with full-color photos. Hard cover, 5½ x 8″, 96 pp.

Index